The Joyful Gospel of Christ

by Zachary Schertz

Illustrated by Todd L Thomas

Copyright 2018 Schertz Writing, All Rights Resereved

Copyright © 2020 by Zachary Schertz.

ISBN-978-1-6485-8874-7

All rights reserved. No part of this book may be reproduced or transmitted in any form or by any means, electronic or mechanical, including photocopying, recording, or by any information storage and retrieval system, without permission in writing from the copyright owner.

The views expressed in this work are solely those of the author and do not necessarily reflect the views of the publisher, and the publisher hereby disclaims any responsibility for them.

Matchstick Literary
1-888-306-8885
orders@matchliterary.com

DEDICATED:

In loving memory to Annie Schertz

Devout Mother and Grandmother

Foreword

"Son of man, speak to the children of thy people, and say unto them, When I bring the sword upon a land, if the people of the land take a man of their coasts, and set him for their Watchman:
If when he seeth the sword come upon the land, he blow the trumpet, and warn the people; then whosoever heareth the sound of the trumpet, and taketh not warning; if the sword come, and take him away, his blood shall be upon his own head. He heard the sound of the trumpet, and took not warning; his blood shall be upon him. But he that taketh warning shall deliver his soul. But if the Watchman see the sword come, and blow not the trumpet, and the people be not warned; if the sword come, and take any person from among them, he is taken away in his iniquity; but his blood will I require at the Watchman's hand."

-Ezekiel 33:2-6

I believe that God has charged me with the mission of being a diligent Watchman. To fulfill this work, I want to honor The Lord in all that I do.

Too many young people are leaving the Church and the primary reason that they are is because they are not being taught The Word. We actually see a direct correlation between youth that remain in the Church and those that were taught that they can trust and stand of The Truth of The Bible alone.

I would argue that if parents taught youths that The Word was history and not just a book of morality they would stay.

If teachers taught their students that Christ and the prophets that foresaw Him were not just good moral examples, but true people they would stay.

If pastors would teach that Christ was more than just a man and just a teacher, they would stay.

Why are young people leaving the Church? Because they do not know who He is.

With the stroke of a pen, I intend to change that and show The Truth of Jesus Christ.

I have a degree in Religious and Theological Studies from St. Edwards University in Austin, Texas and started planning this project back when I was still in college. I hope that you can use this to help you grow in your own faith journey.

This book is designed to supplement The Bible and I have put all of the scripture citations at the very back. Please use them to help understand The Good Book all the more. We know that there is not a contradiction in The Bible. However, people that hate The Lord read this work, not for their souls, but to look for contradictions. Building on the work of men wiser than myself, I am attempting to show that there are no contradictions.

The Evangelists wrote to save souls and were more focused on that than the timeline as such, there only appears to be contradictions. Trust in The Good Book first and everything else will fall into place.

-Zachary James Schertz

What can I ever be but a Lover of God? It was not I who chose Him, but He who chose me. And for what, I am only beginning to understand. For fellowship... for sharing in the beauty of all that He is. And why was I practically born with brushes in hand, paints, canvas and easel before me? To capture all that He is and share it with the world, so it seems. And that is not all. For these talents, they are His. And He, entrust them to those who show themselves faithful, He will surely endow with more... and so there are... the many facets of all that He is... the height, depth, width and length of Almighty God, our Creator, being poured out freely to those will invest them for His interest, for His Glory.

And so it is... that I present my best in this, to present the birth of God's best... to the world... with joy in my heart... a sort of dream come true for me, to visually present a truthful depiction of the Gospel. What an honor, what a privilege. A special thanks to Zachary Schertz for this opportunity.

Lord, Bless this Mission of The Gospel into the heart and souls of those who receive it... that they might know You, and be known by You. Amen.

-Todd L. Thomas

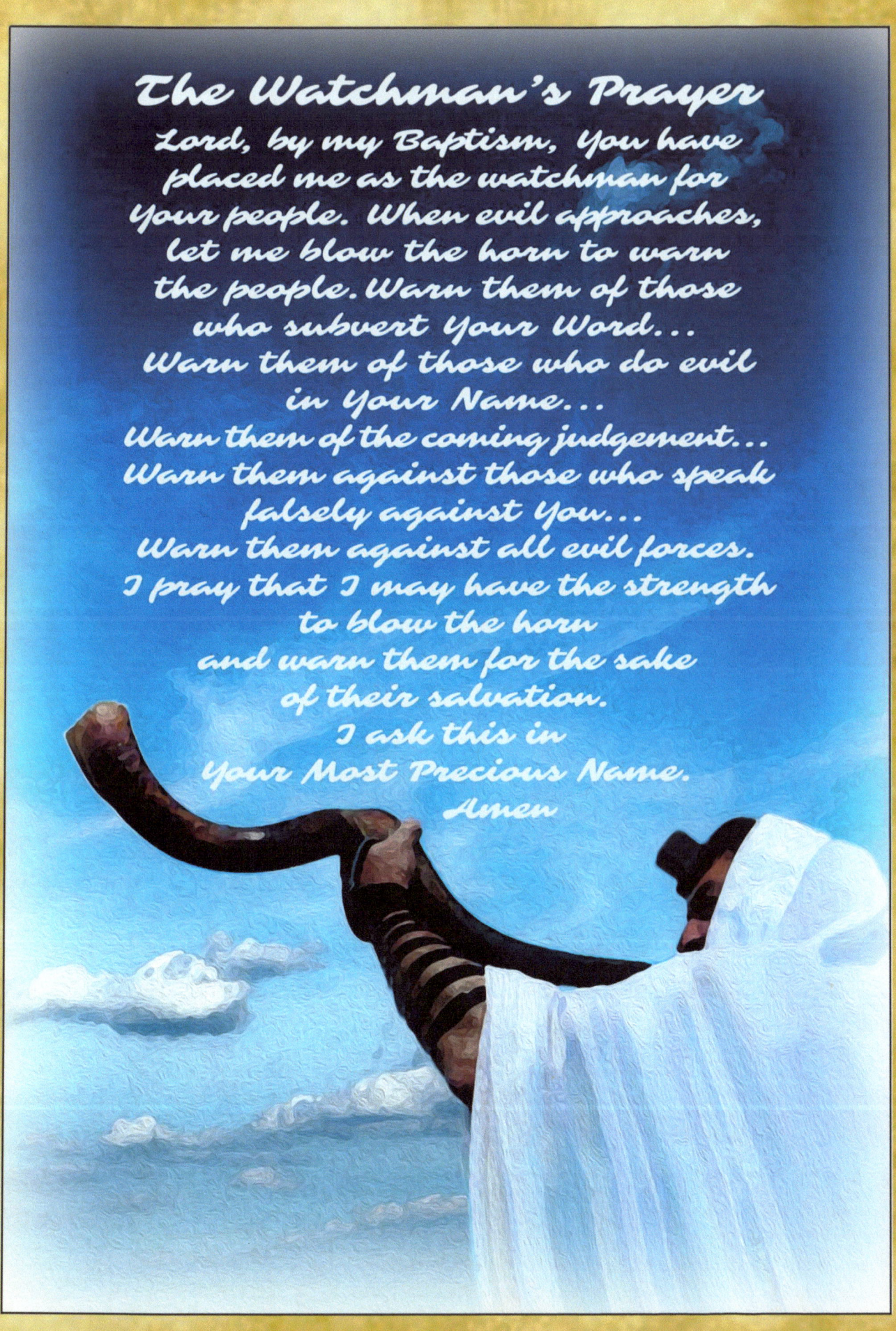

The Watchman's Prayer

Lord, by my Baptism, You have placed me as the watchman for Your people. When evil approaches, let me blow the horn to warn the people. Warn them of those who subvert Your Word...
Warn them of those who do evil in Your Name...
Warn them of the coming judgement...
Warn them against those who speak falsely against You...
Warn them against all evil forces.
I pray that I may have the strength to blow the horn
and warn them for the sake of their salvation.
I ask this in
Your Most Precious Name.
Amen

Table of Contents

The Coming of John the Baptist..01

The Annunciation of Christ..06

The Visitation of Mary..11

The Birth of John the Baptist..15

Mary's Return to Nazareth...20

The Nativity of Our Lord..22

The Presentation of Christ in The Temple..26

The Magi Adore Christ...30

The Flight to Egypt...34

The Finding of Jesus in The Temple..38

The Ministry of John The Baptist..41

Map of The Holy Land..47

Source Citations..48

Appendix..53

Index...57

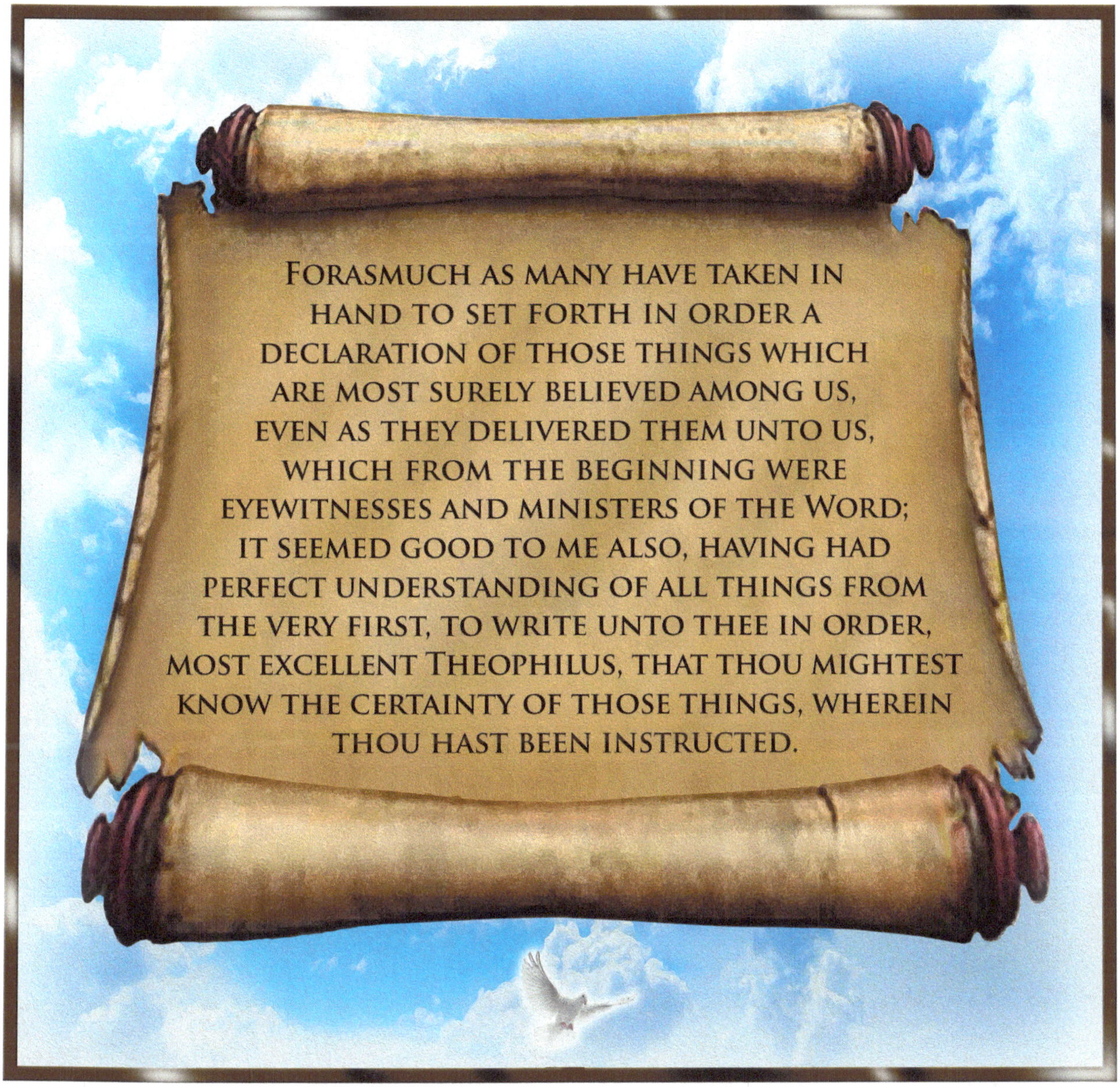

Forasmuch as many have taken in hand to set forth in order a declaration of those things which are most surely believed among us, even as they delivered them unto us, which from the beginning were eyewitnesses and ministers of the Word; it seemed good to me also, having had perfect understanding of all things from the very first, to write unto thee in order, most excellent Theophilus, that thou mightest know the certainty of those things, wherein thou hast been instructed.

There was in the days of Herod, the king of Judaea, a certain priest named Zacharias, of the course of Abia...

And his wife was of the daughters of Aaron, and her name was Elisabeth.

They were both righteous before God, walking in all the commandments and ordinances of The Lord blameless.

They had no child, because that Elisabeth was barren, and they both were now well stricken in years.

It came to pass, that while he executed the priest's office before God in the order of his course, according to the custom of the priest's office, his lot was to burn incense when he went into The Temple of The Lord.

The whole multitude of the people were praying...

...At the time of incense.

And there appeared unto him an Angel of The Lord standing on the right side of the altar of incense. And when Zacharias saw him, he was troubled, and fear fell upon him.

Gabriel: Fear not, Zacharias, for thy prayer is heard and thy wife Elisabeth shall bear thee a son…

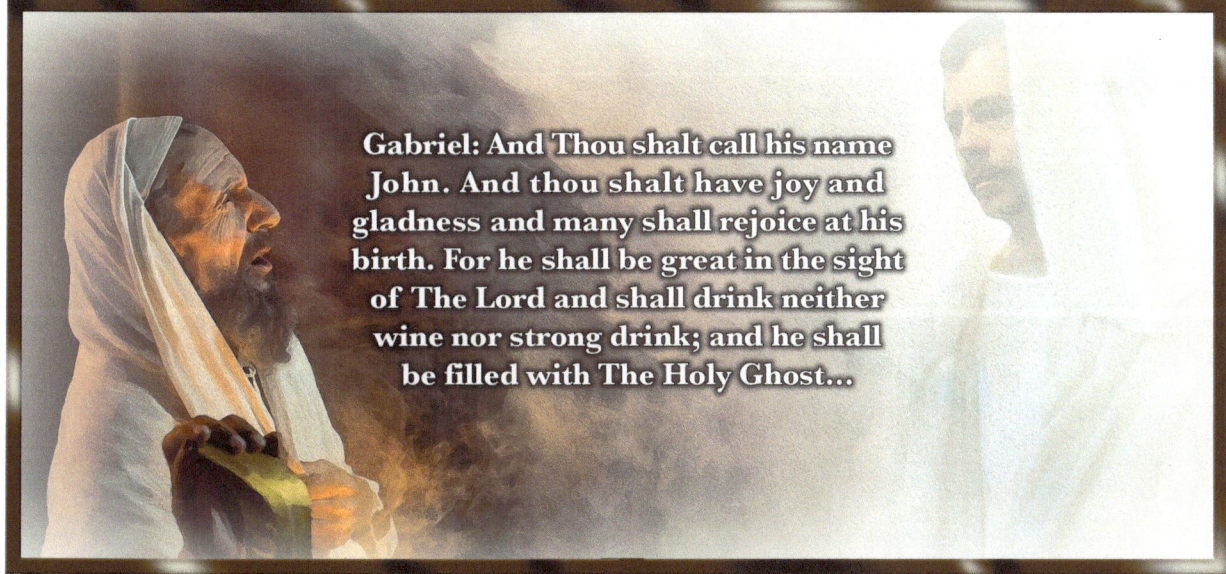

Gabriel: And Thou shalt call his name John. And thou shalt have joy and gladness and many shall rejoice at his birth. For he shall be great in the sight of The Lord and shall drink neither wine nor strong drink; and he shall be filled with The Holy Ghost…

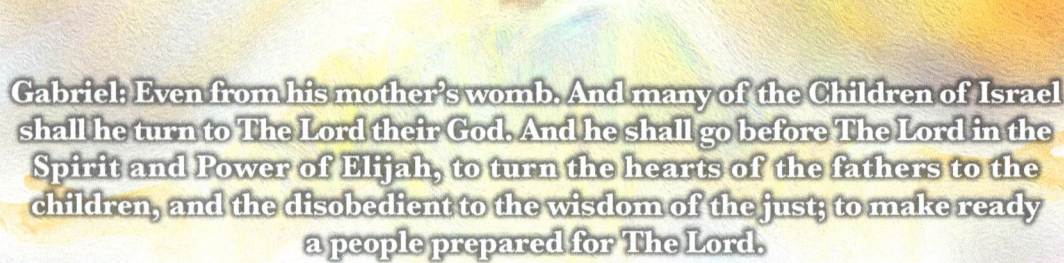

Gabriel: Even from his mother's womb. And many of the Children of Israel shall he turn to The Lord their God. And he shall go before The Lord in the Spirit and Power of Elijah, to turn the hearts of the fathers to the children, and the disobedient to the wisdom of the just; to make ready a people prepared for The Lord.

Zacharias: Whereby shall I know this? For I am an old man, and my wife well stricken in years.

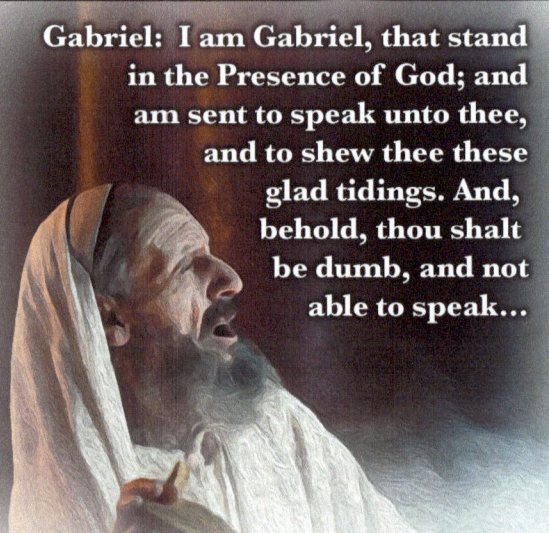

Gabriel: I am Gabriel, that stand in the Presence of God; and am sent to speak unto thee, and to shew thee these glad tidings. And, behold, thou shalt be dumb, and not able to speak…

Gabriel: Until the day that these things shall be performed, because thou believest not my words…

Gabriel: Which shall be fulfilled in their season.

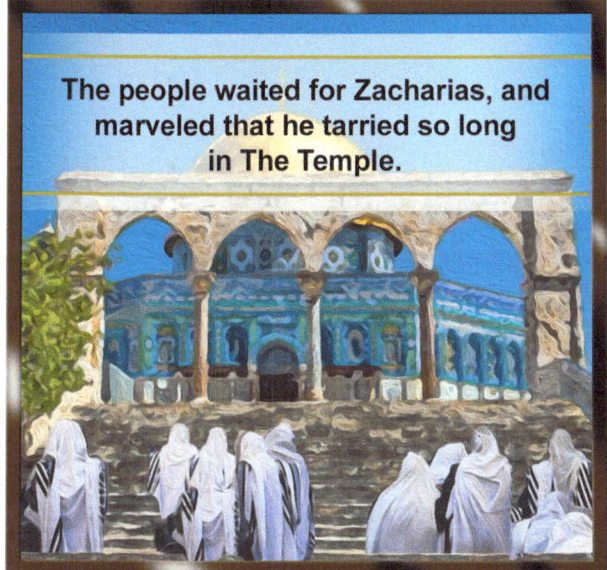

The people waited for Zacharias, and marveled that he tarried so long in The Temple.

They percieved that he had seen a Vision in The Temple...

For he beckoned unto them, and remained speechless.

It came to pass, that, as soon as the days of his ministration were accomplished, he departed to his own house.

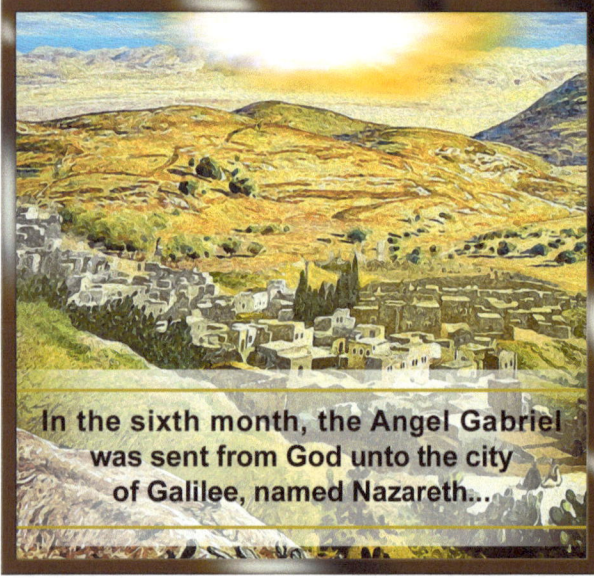

Gabriel: The Lord God shall give unto Him the throne of His father David. And He Shall reign over the House of Jacob forever; and of His Kingdom there shall be no end.

Mary: How shall this be, seeing I know not a man?

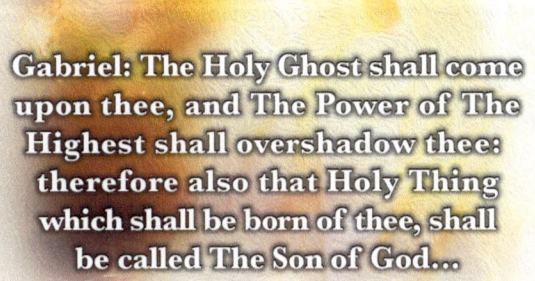

Gabriel: The Holy Ghost shall come upon thee, and The Power of The Highest shall overshadow thee: therefore also that Holy Thing which shall be born of thee, shall be called The Son of God…

Mary arose in those days, and went into the hill country with haste...

Into a city of Judah...

And entered into the house of Zacharias.

Elisabeth: Blessed art thou among women, and blessed is the Fruit of thy womb.

Elisabeth: And whence is this to me, that the mother of my Lord should come to me?

Mary: He hath shewed Strength with His Arm; He hath scattered the proud in the imagination of their hearts.

Mary: He hath put down the mighty from their seats, and exalted them of low degree. He hath filled the hungry with good things; and the rich He hath sent away empty.

Mary: He hath helped His servant Israel, in remembrance of His Mercy; as He spake to our fathers, to Abraham, and to his seed forever.

Mary abode with her about three months, and returned to her own house.

Now Elisabeth's full time came that she should be delivered; and she brought forth a son. And her neighbours and her cousins heard how The Lord had shewed great mercy upon her; and they rejoiced with her...

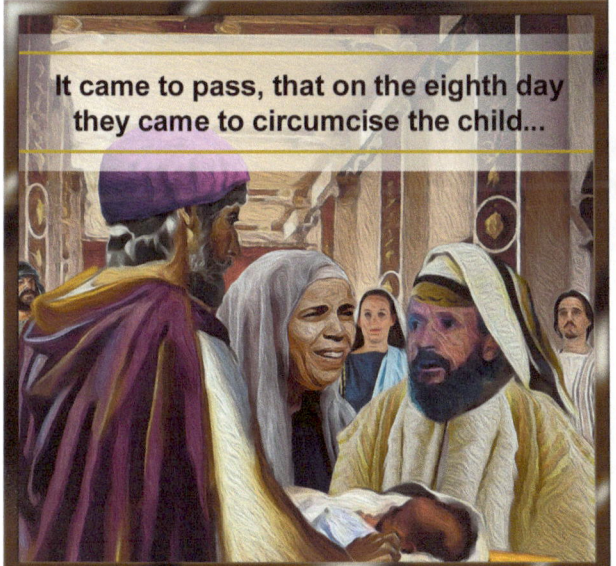

It came to pass, that on the eighth day they came to circumcise the child...

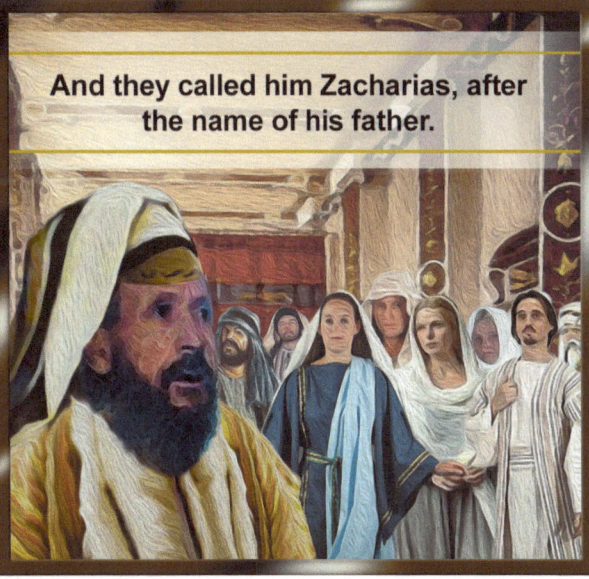

And they called him Zacharias, after the name of his father.

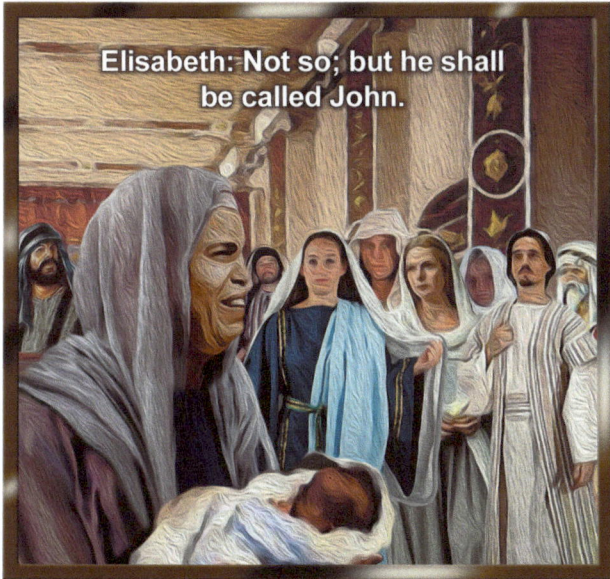

Elisabeth: Not so; but he shall be called John.

Neighbors: There is none of thy kindred that is called by this name.

And they made signs to his father, Zacharias, how he would have him called.

And he asked for a writing table, and wrote, saying, "His name is John" And they marvelled all.

Zacharias: Blessed be The Lord God of Israel; for He hath visited and redeemed His people, and hath raised up an horn of salvation for us in the house of His servant David...

Zacharias: As He spake by the mouth of His holy prophets, which have been since the world began; That we should be saved from our enemies, and from the hand of all that hate us; to perform the mercy promised to our fathers, and to remember His Holy Covenant...

Zacharias: The oath which He sware to our father Abraham, that He would grant unto us, that we being delivered out of the hand of our enemies might serve Him without fear, in holiness and righteousness before Him all the days of our life. And thou, child, shalt be called the Prophet of The Highest: for thou shalt go before The Face of The Lord to prepare His ways; to give knowledge of salvation unto His people...

Zacharias: By the remission of their sins, through the tender mercy of our God; whereby The Dayspring from on High hath visited us, to give light to them in darkness and in the shadow of death, to guide our feet into the way of peace.

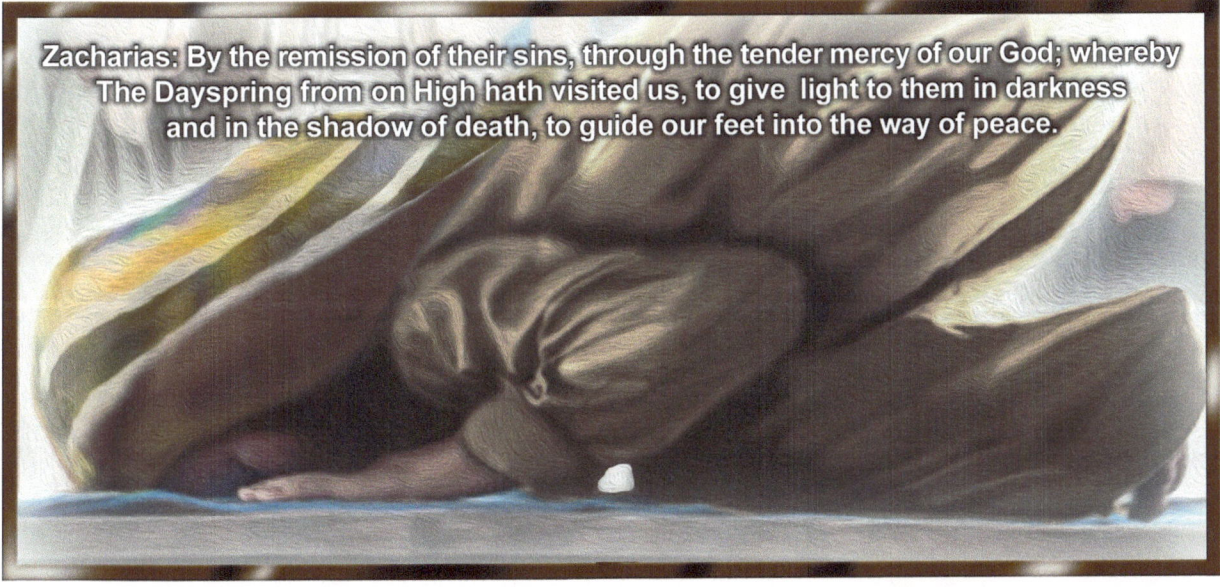

John grew, and waxed strong in spirit...

And the same John had his raiment of camel's hair and a leathern belt about his waist; and his meat was locusts and wild honey...

And was in the deserts till the day of his shewing unto Israel.

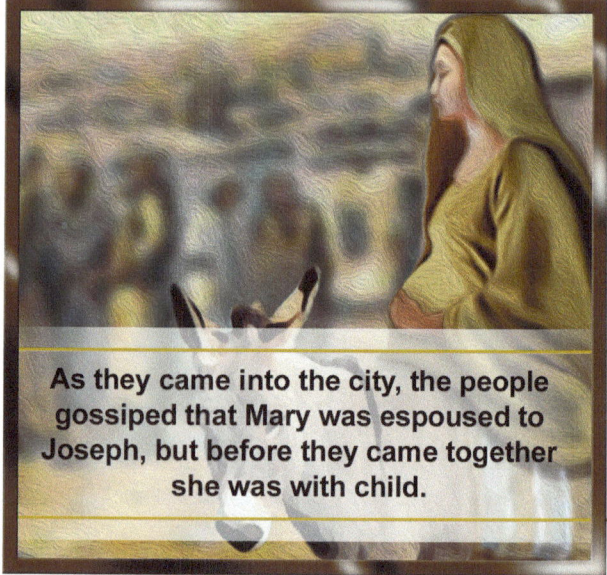

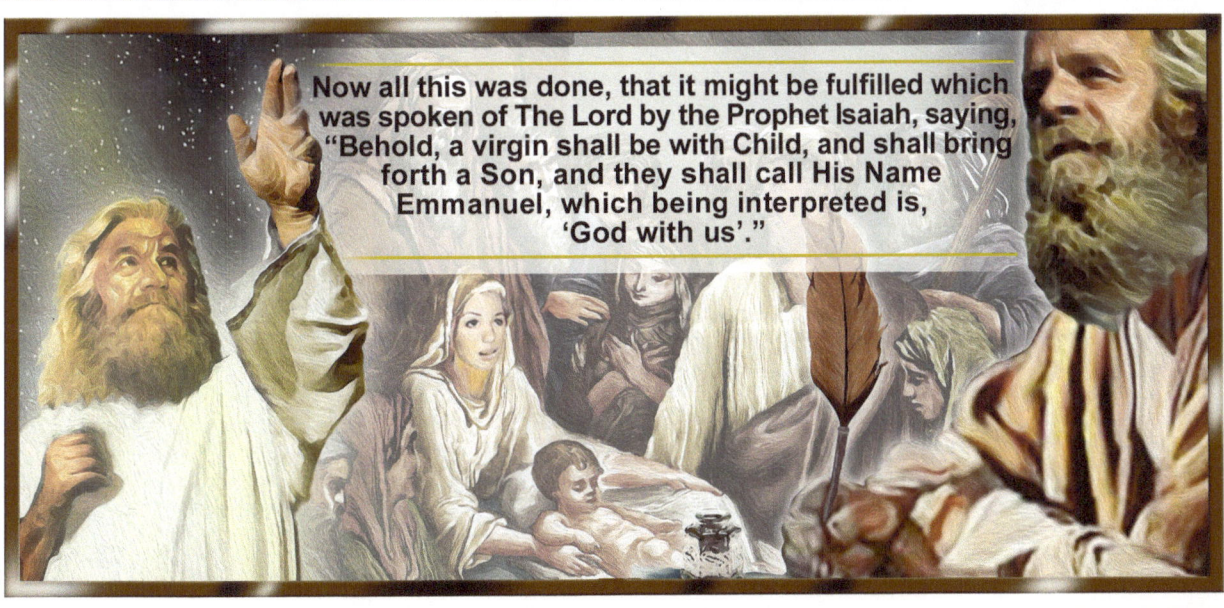

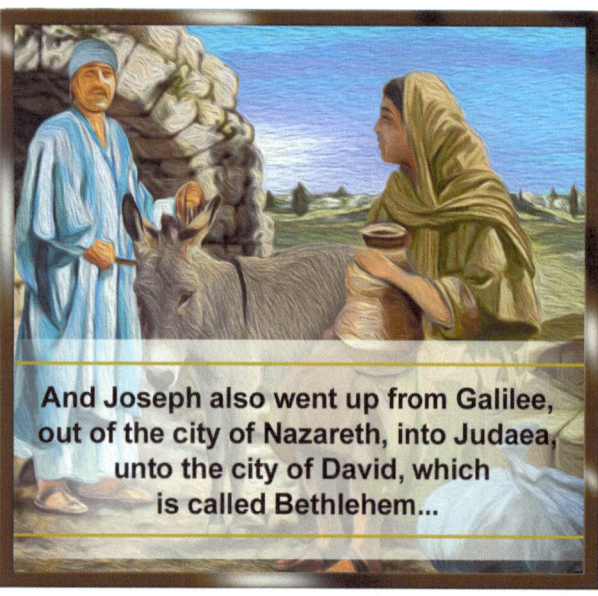

Because there was no room for them in the house.

And there were in the same country, shepherds, abiding in the field, keeping watch over their flock by night.

And lo, the Angel of the Lord came upon them, and The Glory of The Lord shone round about them: and they were sore afraid.

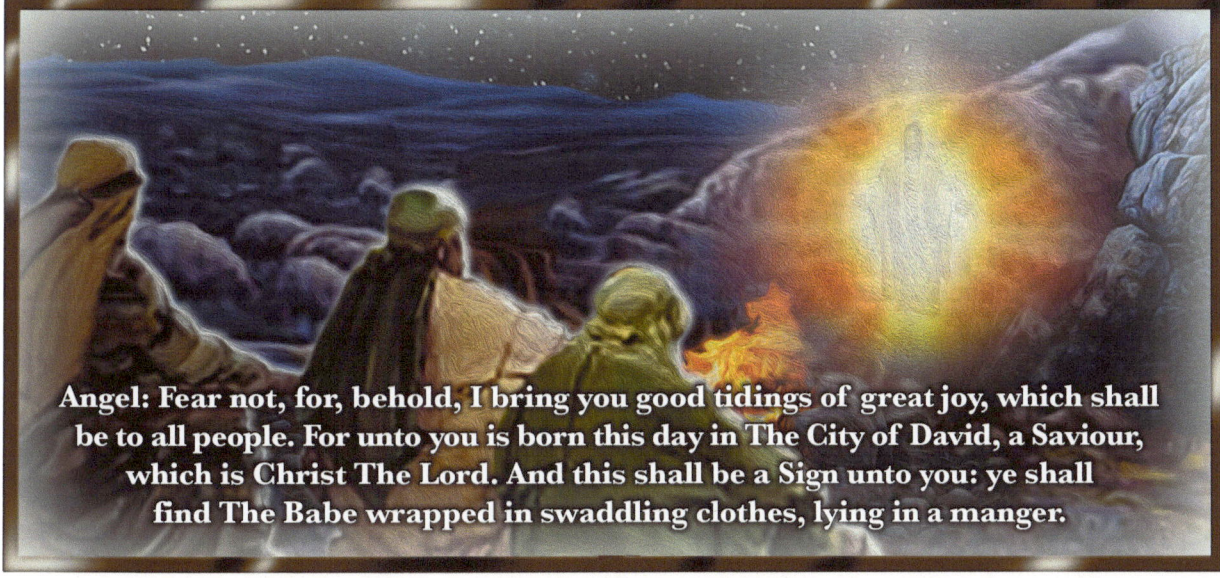

Angel: Fear not, for, behold, I bring you good tidings of great joy, which shall be to all people. For unto you is born this day in The City of David, a Saviour, which is Christ The Lord. And this shall be a Sign unto you: ye shall find The Babe wrapped in swaddling clothes, lying in a manger.

Suddenly there was with The Angel a multitude of the Heavenly Host praising God, and saying, "Glory to God in The Highest, and on Earth, peace, good will toward men."

And it came to pass, as the Angels were gone away from them into Heaven, the shepherds said one to another, "Let us now go even unto Bethlehem, and see this thing which is come to pass, which The Lord hath made known unto us."

And they came with haste, and found Mary, and Joseph, and The Babe lying in a manger.

When they had seen it, they made known abroad the saying which was told them concerning this Child.

All they that heard it wondered at those things which were told them by the shepherds.

But Mary kept all these things, and pondered them in her heart.

The shepherds returned, glorifying and praising God for all the things that they had heard and seen, as it was told unto them.

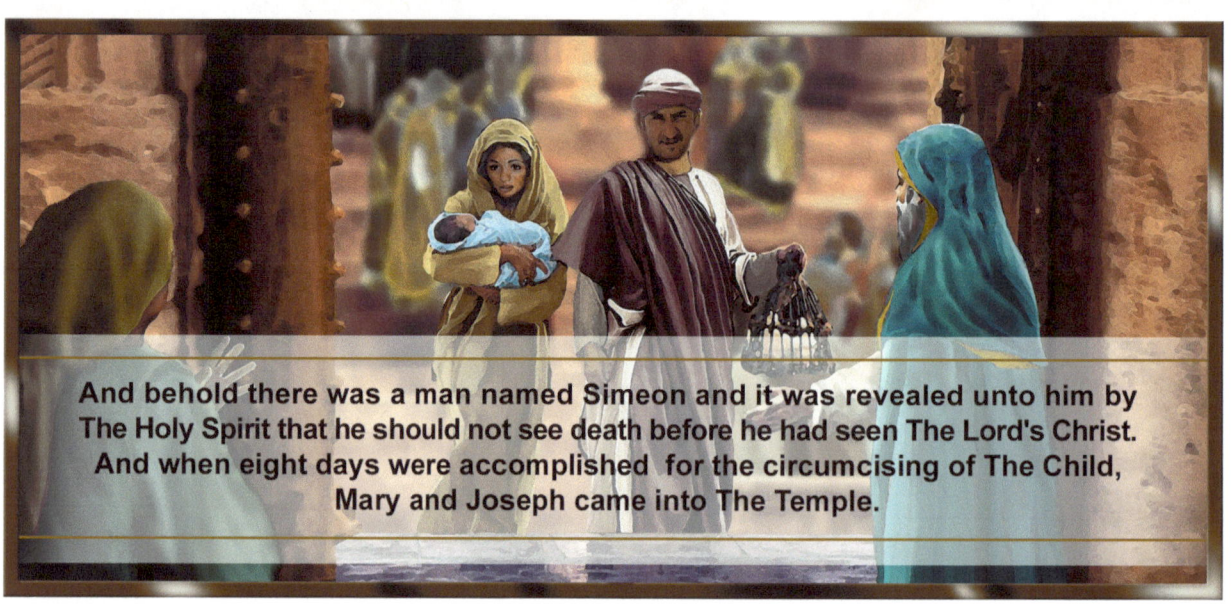

And behold there was a man named Simeon and it was revealed unto him by The Holy Spirit that he should not see death before he had seen The Lord's Christ. And when eight days were accomplished for the circumcising of The Child, Mary and Joseph came into The Temple.

Simeon: Lord, now lettest thou thy servant depart in peace, according to Thy Word: For mine eyes have seen Thy Salvation, which Thou hast prepared before the face of all people; A Light to lighten the Gentiles, and the glory of Thy people Israel.

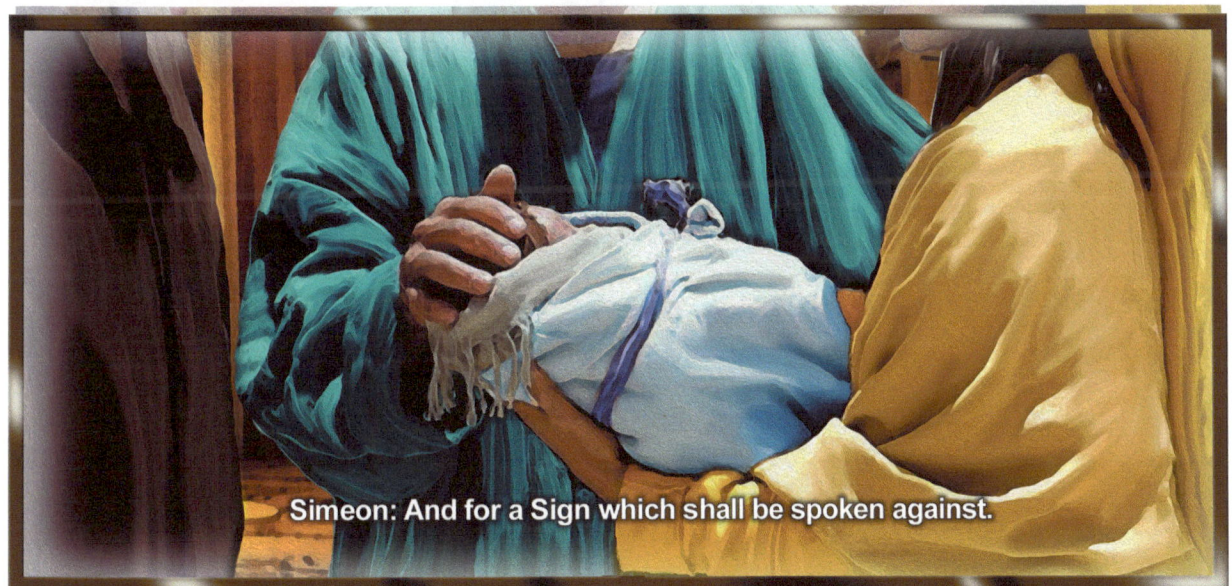
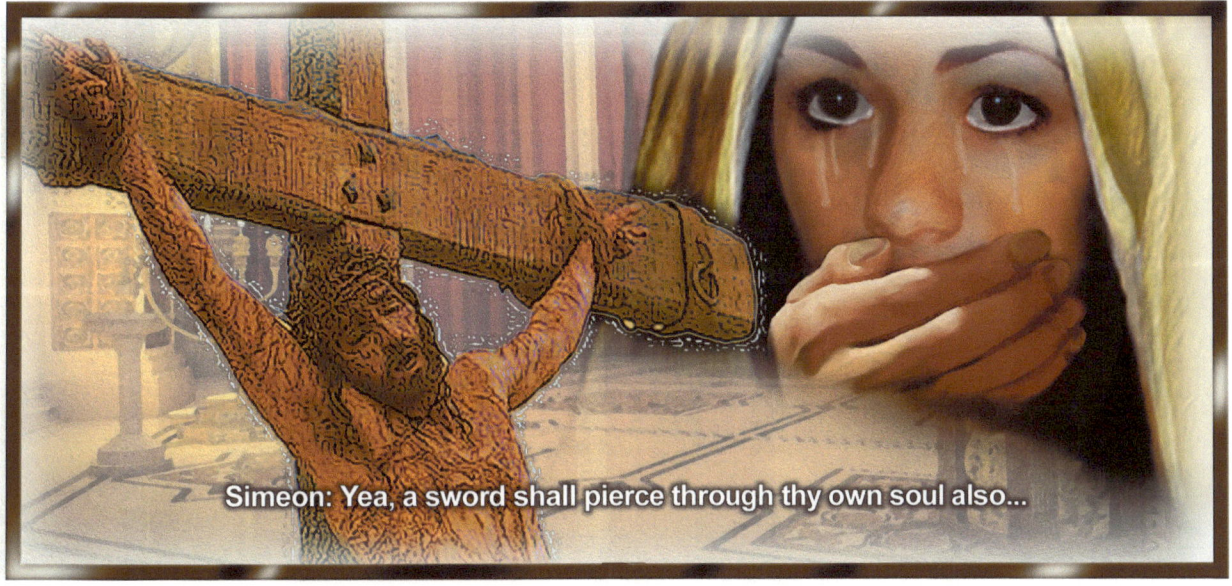

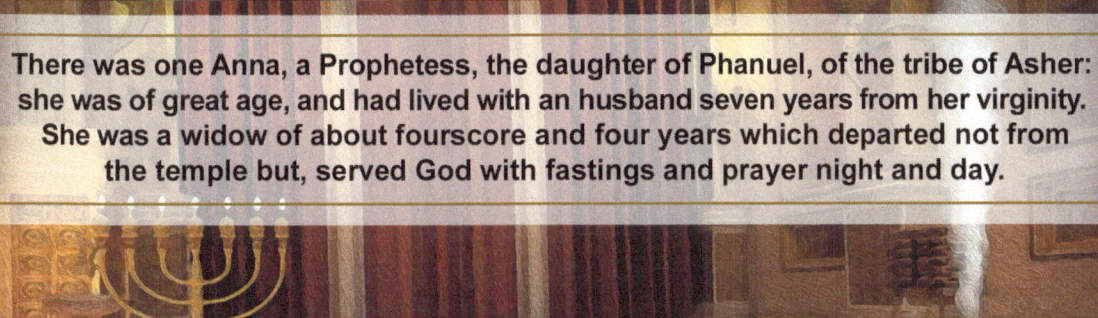

There was one Anna, a Prophetess, the daughter of Phanuel, of the tribe of Asher: she was of great age, and had lived with an husband seven years from her virginity. She was a widow of about fourscore and four years which departed not from the temple but, served God with fastings and prayer night and day.

Coming in that instant gave thanks likewise unto The Lord, and spake of Him to all them that looked for redemption in Jerusalem.

When they had performed all things according to The Law of The Lord, they returned into Galilee, to their own city Nazareth.

Now when Jesus was born in Bethlehem of Judea in the days of Herod the king, behold, there came wise men from the east to Jerusalem.

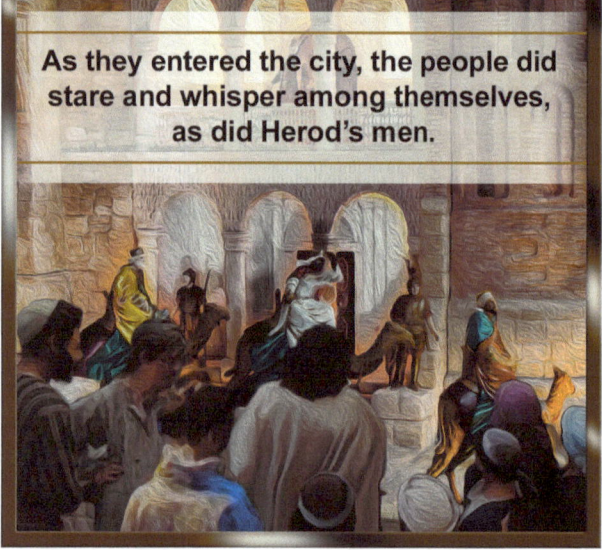

As they entered the city, the people did stare and whisper among themselves, as did Herod's men.

Word was swiftly told to King Herod of their arrival.

Herod: Go and find these men of the East, and bring them to me at once!

And King Herod's men did as commanded and found the Wise Men of the East to bring them before King Herod.

The Wisemen of the East were then brought before King Herod for an audience.

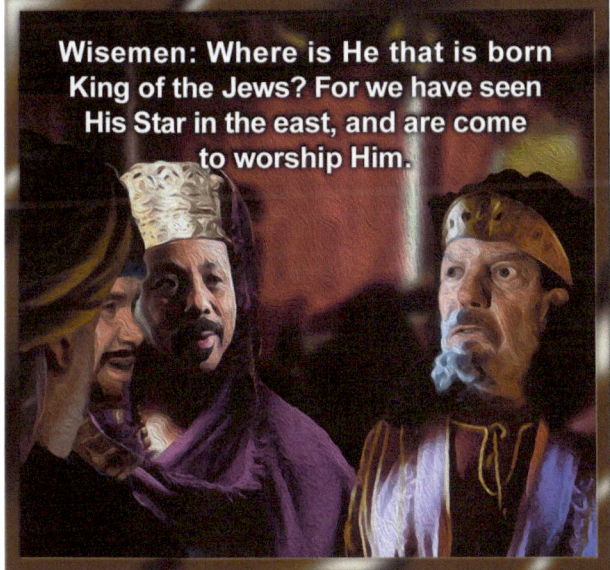
Wisemen: Where is He that is born King of the Jews? For we have seen His Star in the east, and are come to worship Him.

When Herod the king had heard these things, he was troubled...

And all Jerusalem with him.

When he had gathered all the chief priests and scribes of the people together, he demanded of them where Christ should be born.

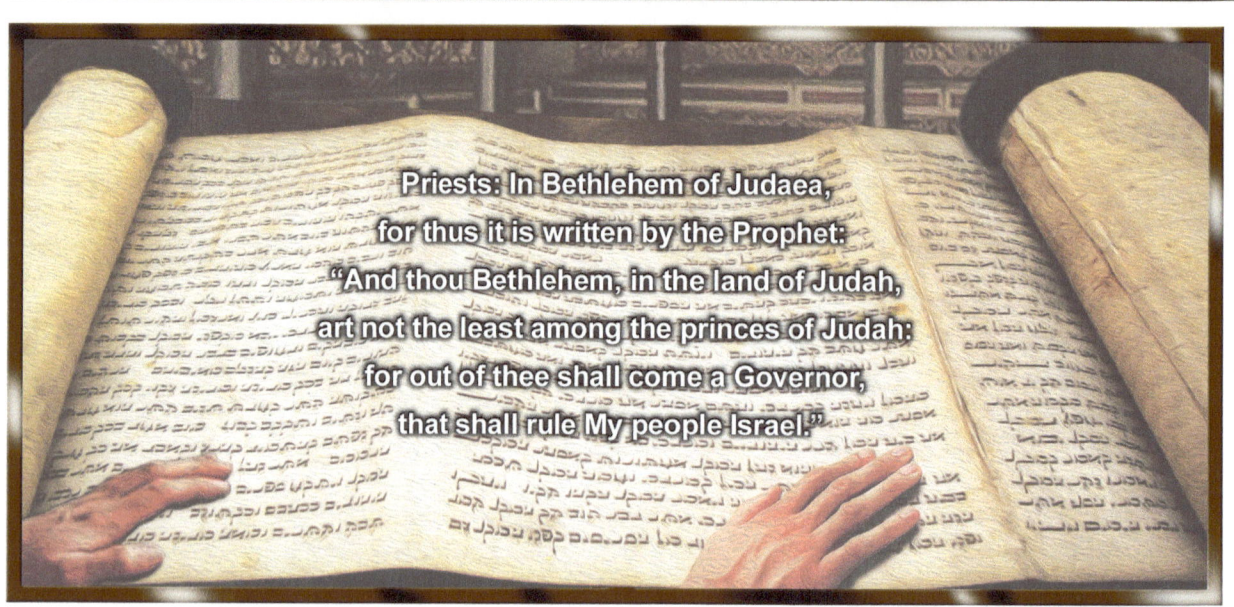

Priests: In Bethlehem of Judaea,
for thus it is written by the Prophet:
"And thou Bethlehem, in the land of Judah,
art not the least among the princes of Judah:
for out of thee shall come a Governor,
that shall rule My people Israel."

Then Herod, when he had privately called the wise men, enquired of them diligently what time the star appeared.

He sent them to Bethlehem.

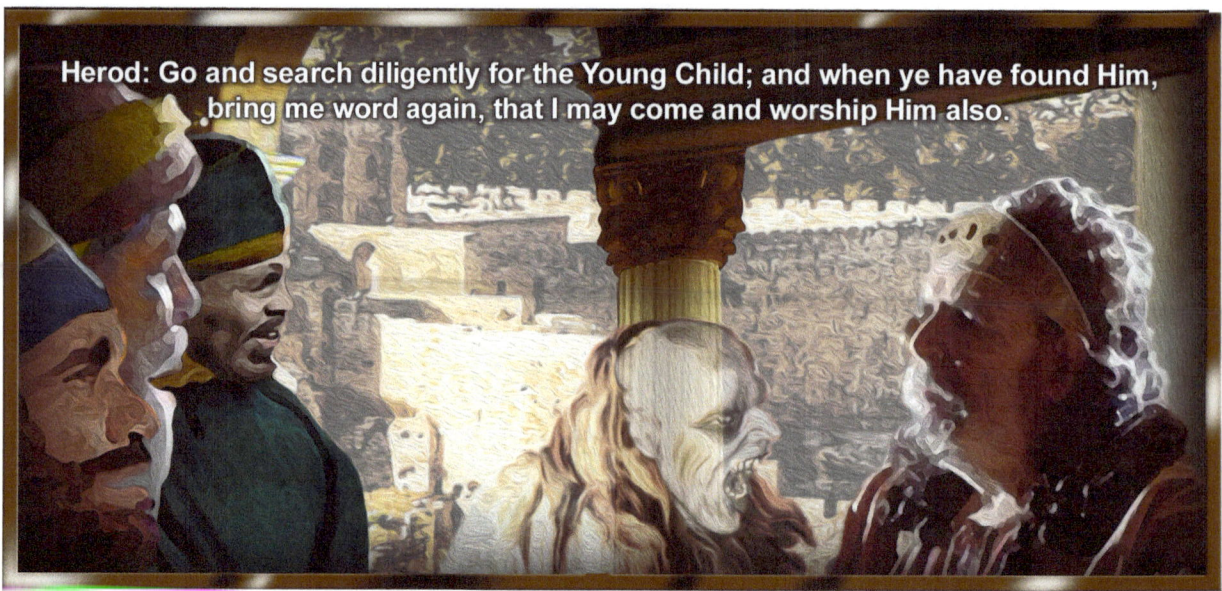

Herod: Go and search diligently for the Young Child; and when ye have found Him, bring me word again, that I may come and worship Him also.

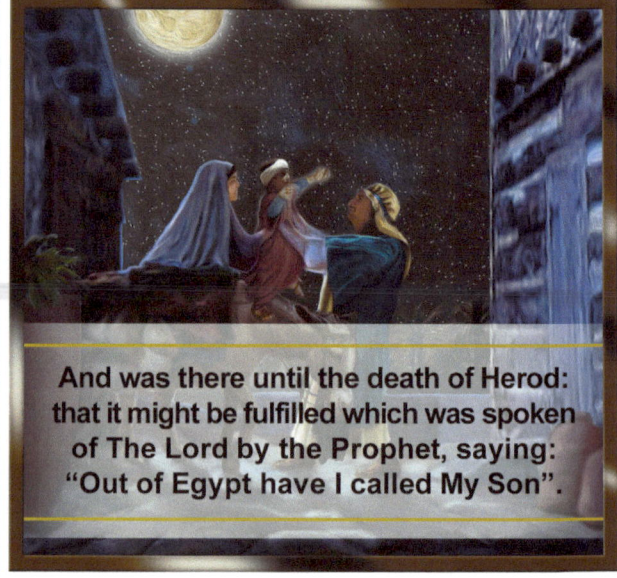

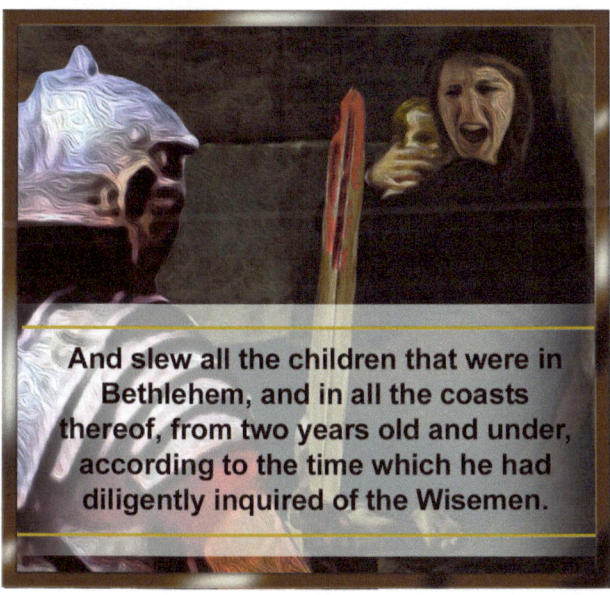
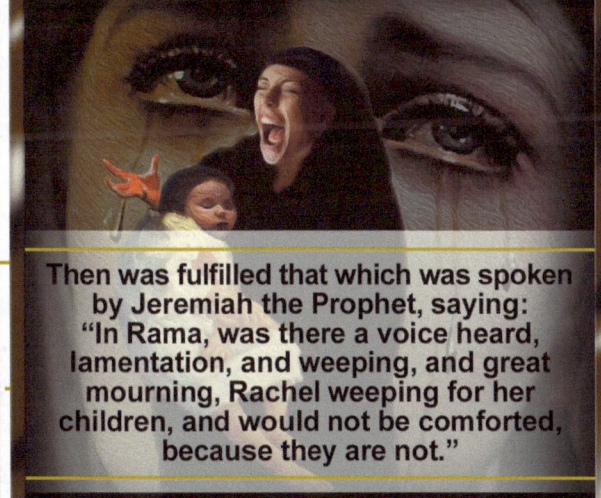
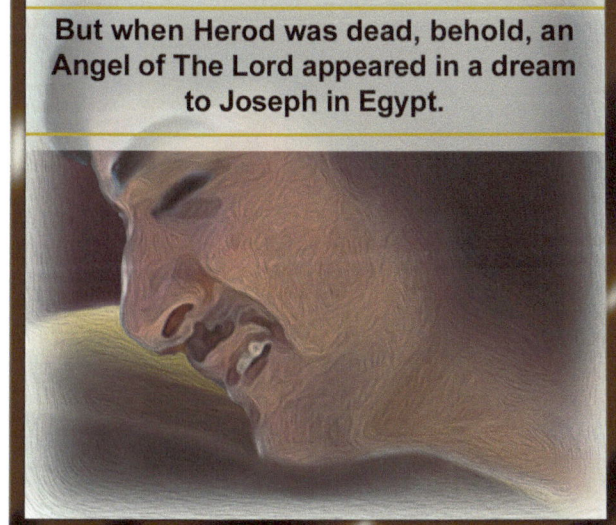
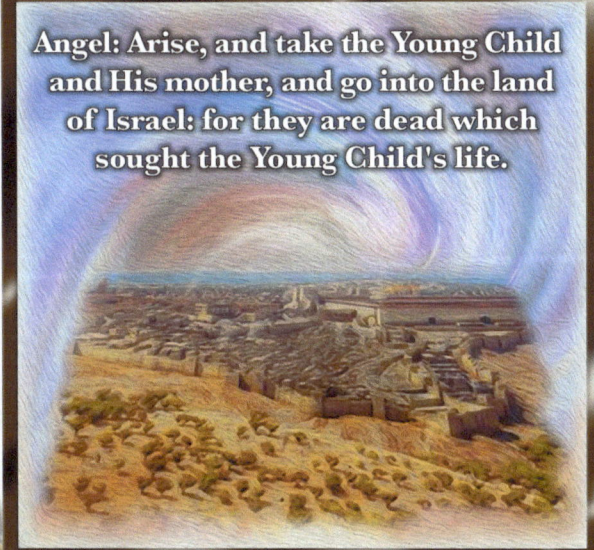

He arose, and took the Young Child and His mother, and came into the land of Israel.

But when he heard that Archelaus did reign in Judaea in the room of his father Herod, he was afraid to go thither...

Notwithstanding, being warned of God in a dream...

He turned aside into the parts of Galilee, and dwelt in a city called Nazareth...

That it might be fulfilled which was spoken by The Prophets: "He shall be called a Nazarene."

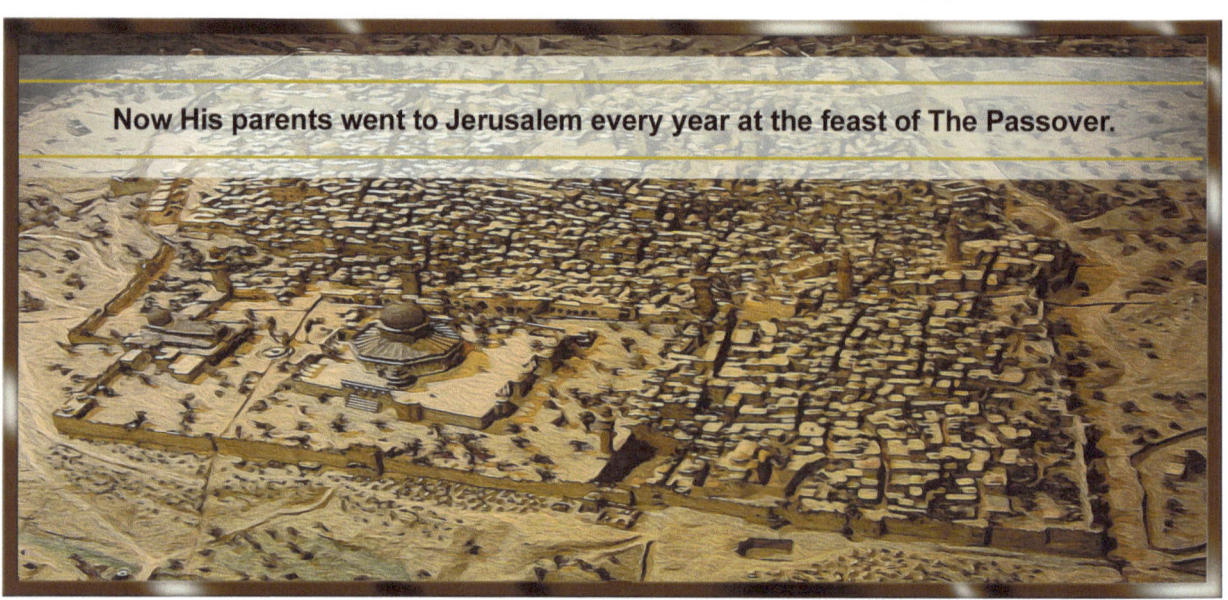

Now His parents went to Jerusalem every year at the feast of The Passover.

When He was twelve years old, they went up to Jerusalem after the custom of the feast.

When they had fulfilled the days, as they returned, The Child Jesus tarried behind in Jerusalem; and Joseph and Mary knew not of it.

But they, supposing Him to have been in the company, went a day's journey; and they sought Him among their kinsfolk and acquaintances. And when they found Him not, they turned back again to Jerusalem, seeking Him.

It came to pass, that after three days they found Him in The Temple, sitting in the midst of the doctors, both hearing them, and asking them questions. And all that heard Him were astonished at His understanding and answers.

Mary: Son, why hast Thou thus dealt with us? Behold, Thy father and I have sought Thee sorrowing.

Jesus: How is it that ye sought Me? Wist ye not that I must be about My Father's Business?

The elders were shocked and talked amongst themselves about this statement.

And His parents understood not the saying which He spake unto them. And He went down with them, and came to Nazareth, and was subject unto them. But His mother kept all these sayings in her heart. Jesus increased in wisdom, stature, and in favour with God and man.

There was a man sent from God, whose name was John. The same came for a witness, to bear witness of The Light that all men through him might believe.

He was not that Light, but was sent to bear witness of that Light. That was The True Light, which lightest every man that cometh into the world.

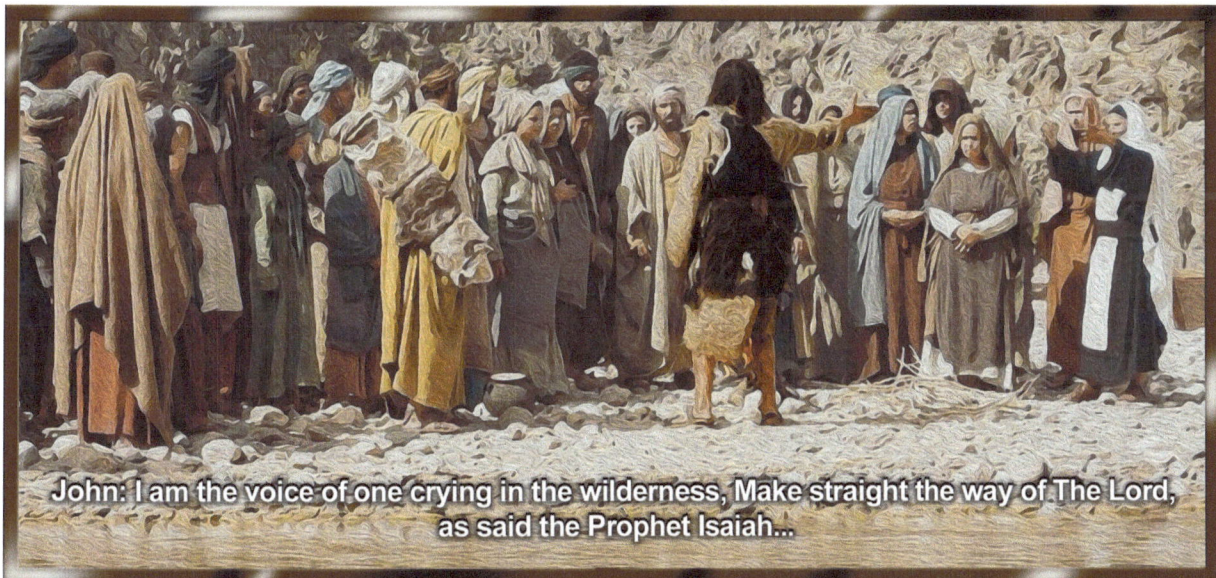

John: I am the voice of one crying in the wilderness, Make straight the way of The Lord, as said the Prophet Isaiah...

John: The voice of one crying in the wilderness: Prepare ye the way of The Lord, make His paths straight. Every valley shall be filled, and every mountain and hill shall be brought low; and the crooked shall be made straight, and the rough ways shall be made smooth; And all flesh shall see the Salvation of God.

And they which were sent were of the Pharisees.

Disciple Of Pharisees: Why baptizest thou then, if thou be not that Christ, nor Elijah, neither that Prophet?

John: I baptize with water: but there standeth One among you, whom ye know not; He it is, who coming after me is preferred before me, whose sandal's latchet I am not worthy to unloose.

Then went out to John, Jerusalem, and all Judaea, and all the region round about Jordan, and were baptized of him in Jordan, confessing their sins.

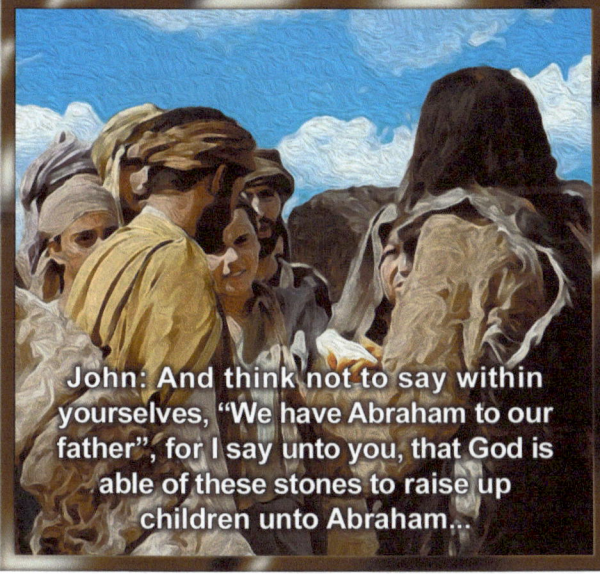

And as the people were in expectation, and all men mused in their hearts of John, whether he were The Christ, or not.

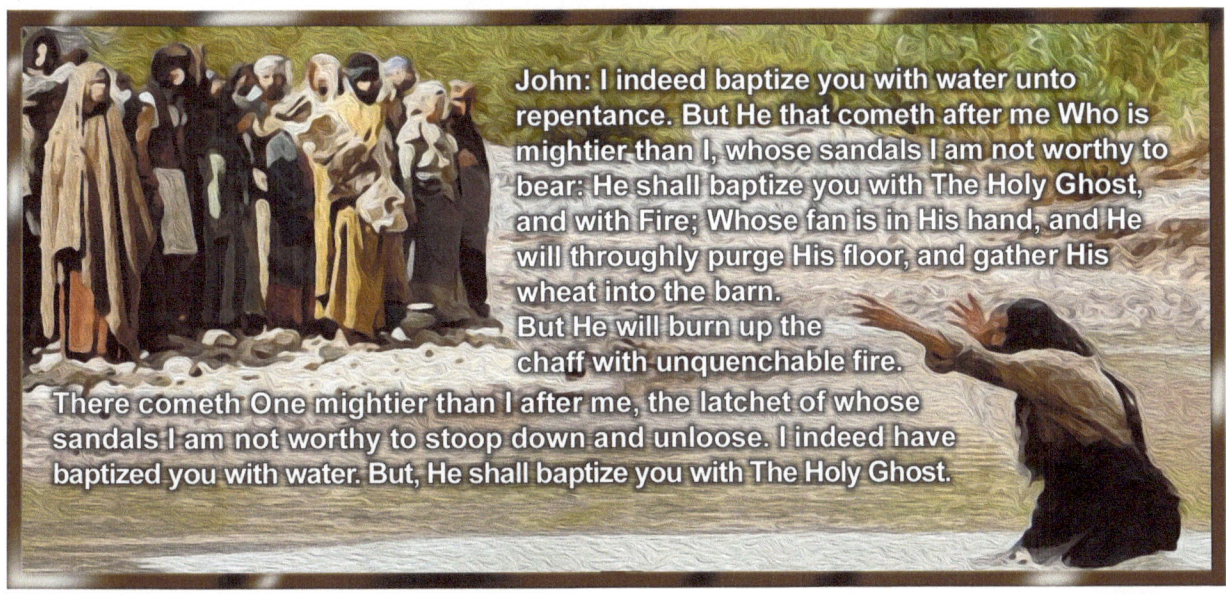

John: I indeed baptize you with water unto repentance. But He that cometh after me Who is mightier than I, whose sandals I am not worthy to bear: He shall baptize you with The Holy Ghost, and with Fire; Whose fan is in His hand, and He will throughly purge His floor, and gather His wheat into the barn.
But He will burn up the chaff with unquenchable fire.
There cometh One mightier than I after me, the latchet of whose sandals I am not worthy to stoop down and unloose. I indeed have baptized you with water. But, He shall baptize you with The Holy Ghost.

COMING UP NEXT

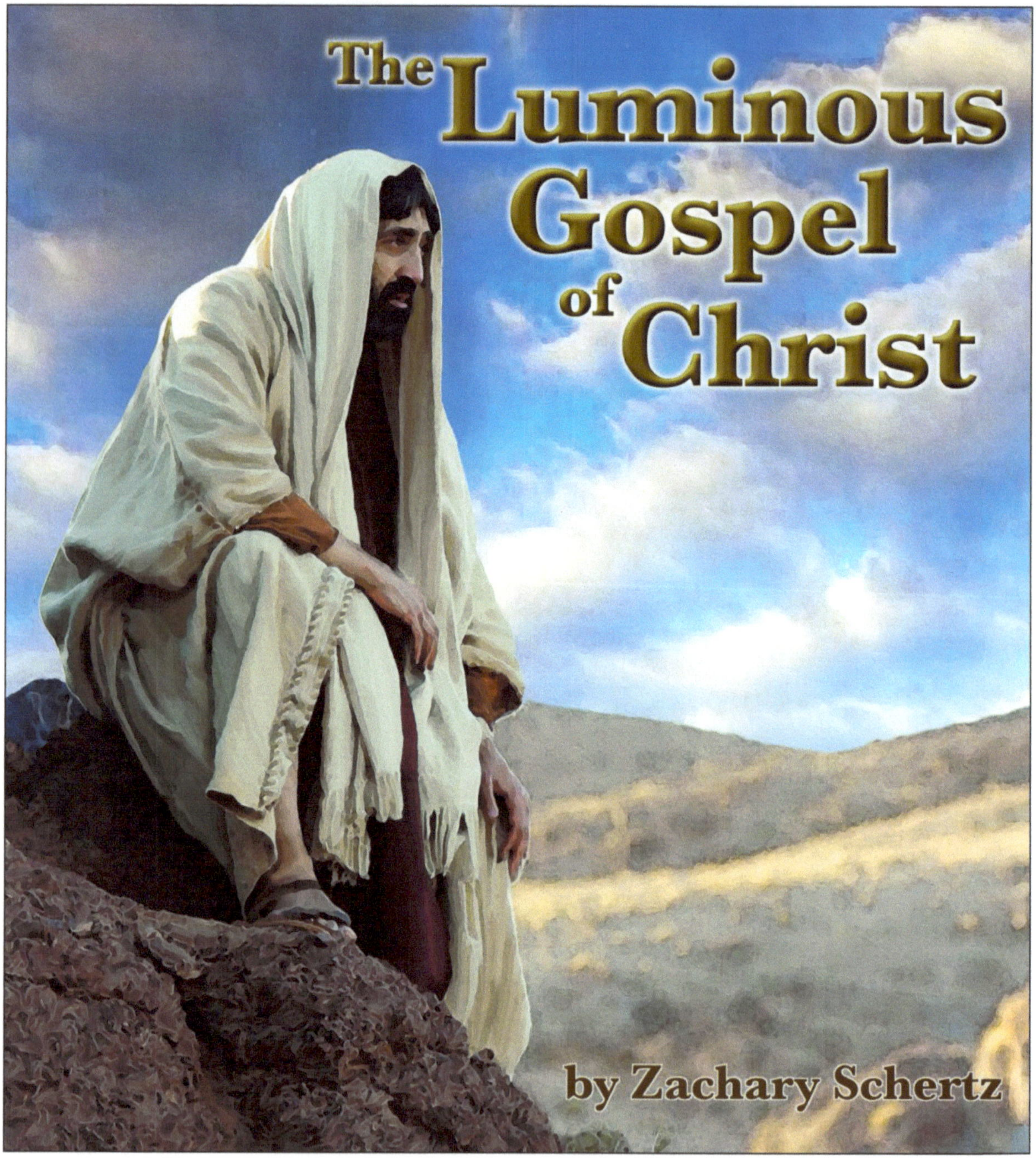

The Luminous Gospel of Christ

by Zachary Schertz

COLLECT THE WHOLE TETRALOGY SET

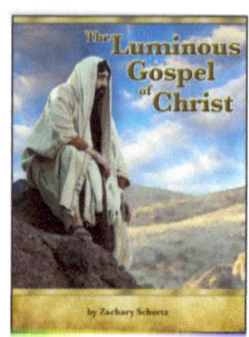

Source Citations

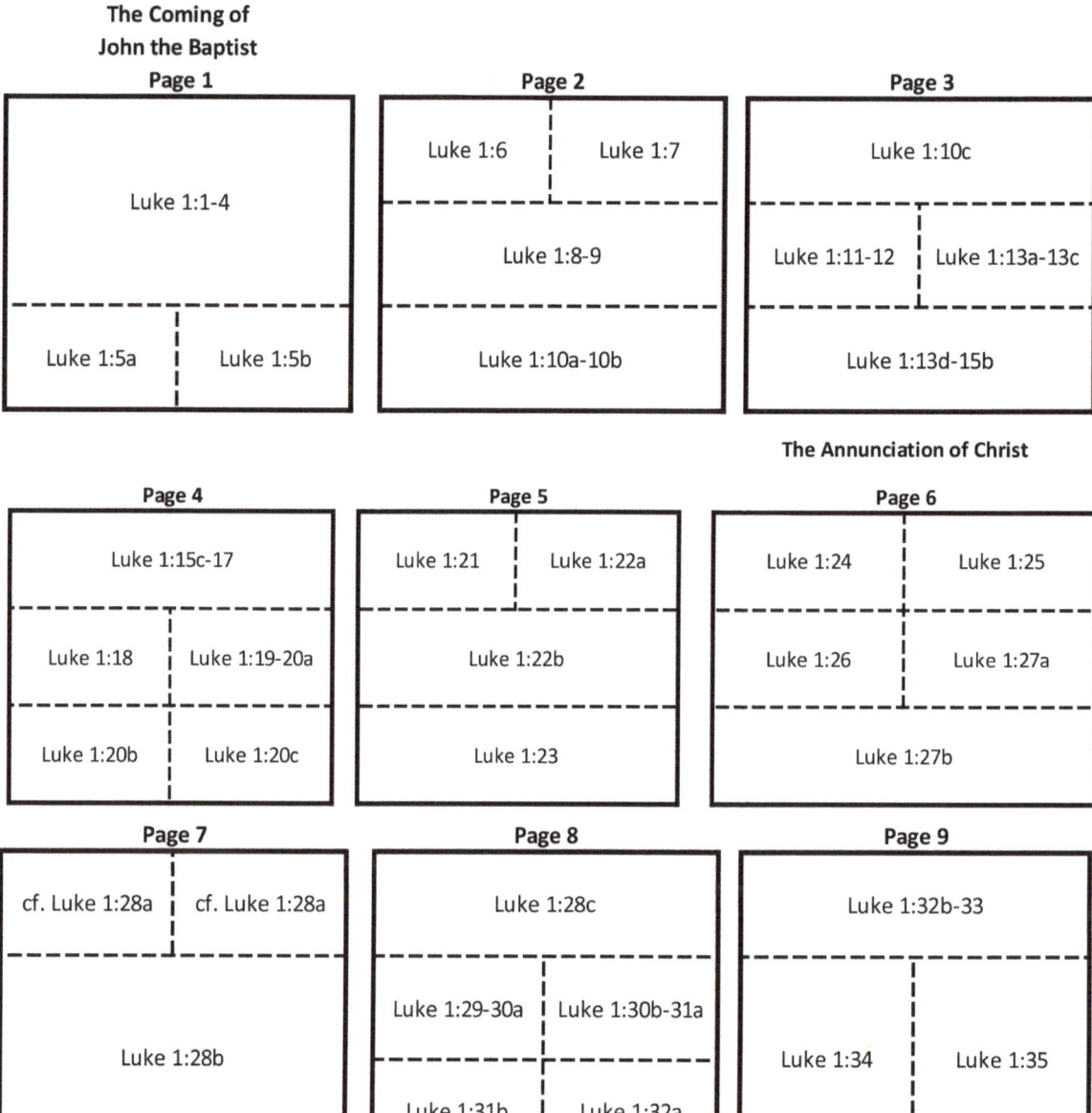

Source Citations

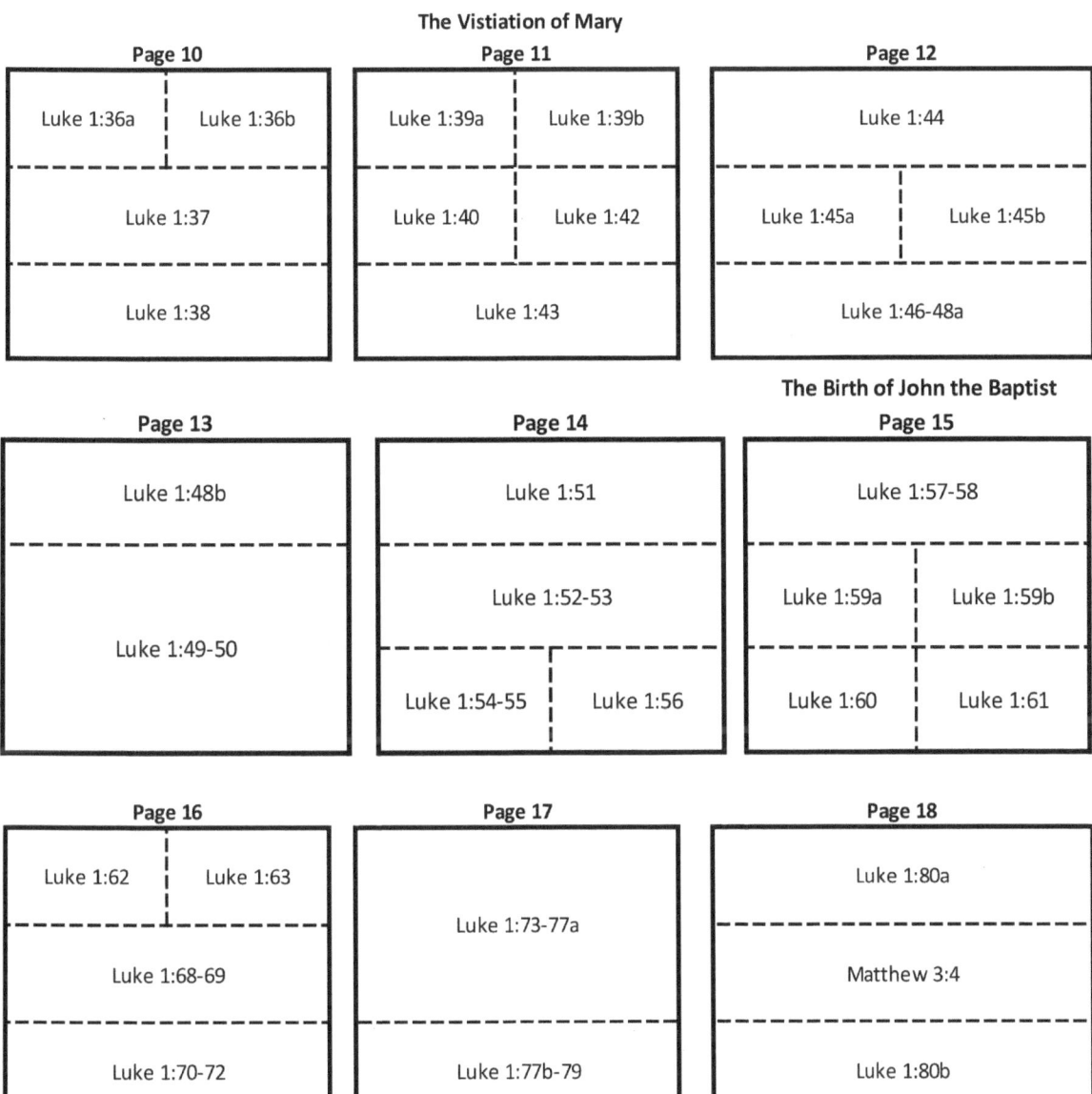

Source Citations

Mary's Return to Nazareth

Page 19

Luke 1:65-66a
Luke 1:66b
Luke 1:66c

Page 20

cf. Matthew 1:18	cf. Matthew 1:18
cf. Matthew 1:18-19	Matthew 1:19
Matthew 1:19	Matthew 1:20

Page 21

Matthew 1:21a	Matthew 1:21b
Matthew 1:24	Matthew 1:25
Matthew 1:22-23	

The Nativity of Our Lord

Page 22

Luke 2:1-2	Luke 2:3
Luke 2:4a	Luke 2:4b-5
Luke 2:6	Luke 2:7a

Page 23

Luke 2:7	
Luke 2:8	Luke 2:9
Luke 2:10-12	

Page 24

Luke 2:13-14
Luke 2:15
Luke 2:16

The Presentation of Christ in The Temple

Page 25

Luke 2:17	
Luke 2:18	Luke 2:19
Luke 2:20	

Page 26

Luke 2:25a Luke 2:26 Luke 2:21a
Luke 2:29-32

Page 27

Luke 2:34a
Luke 2:34b
Luke 2:35

Source Citations

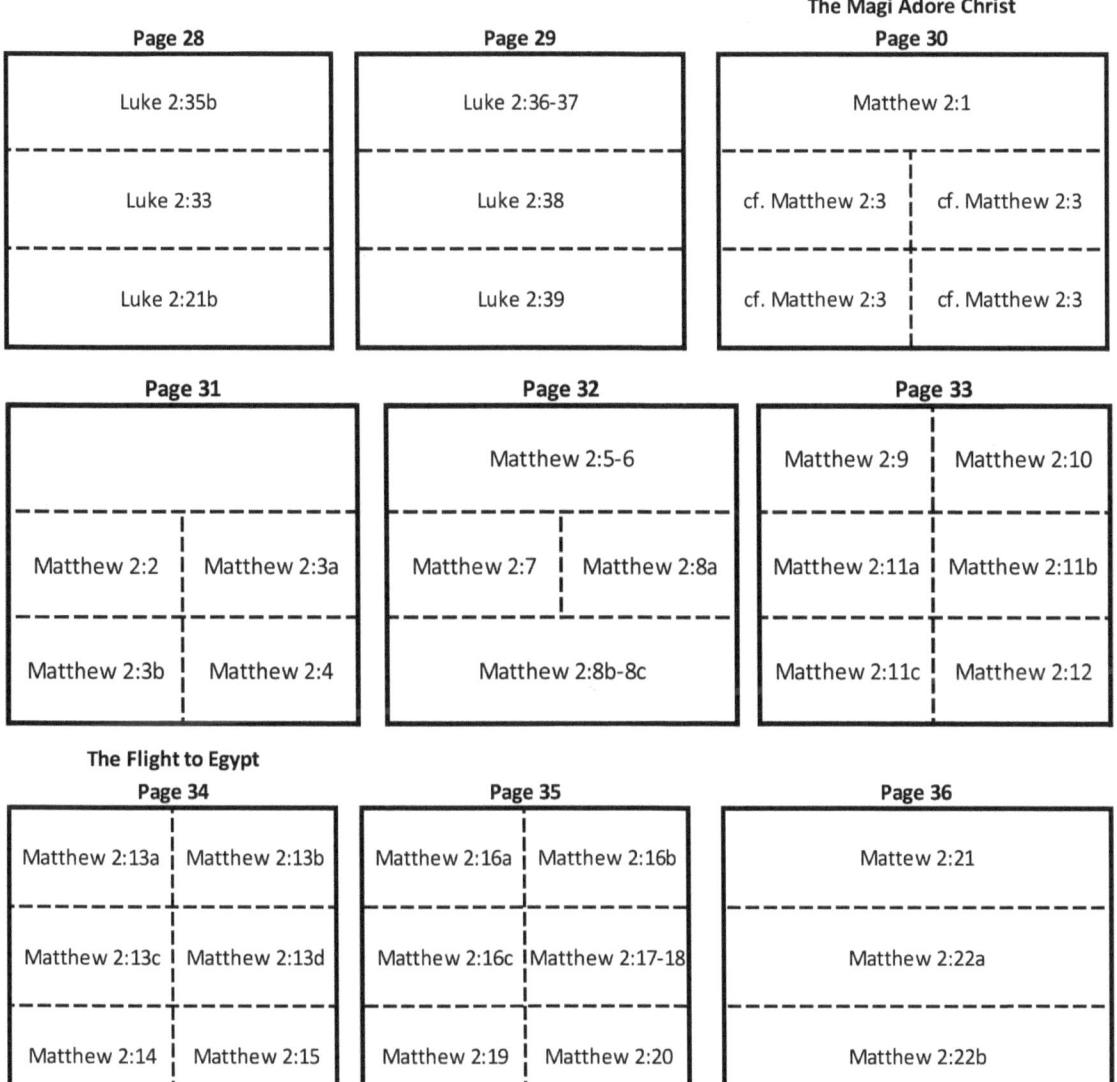

Source Citations

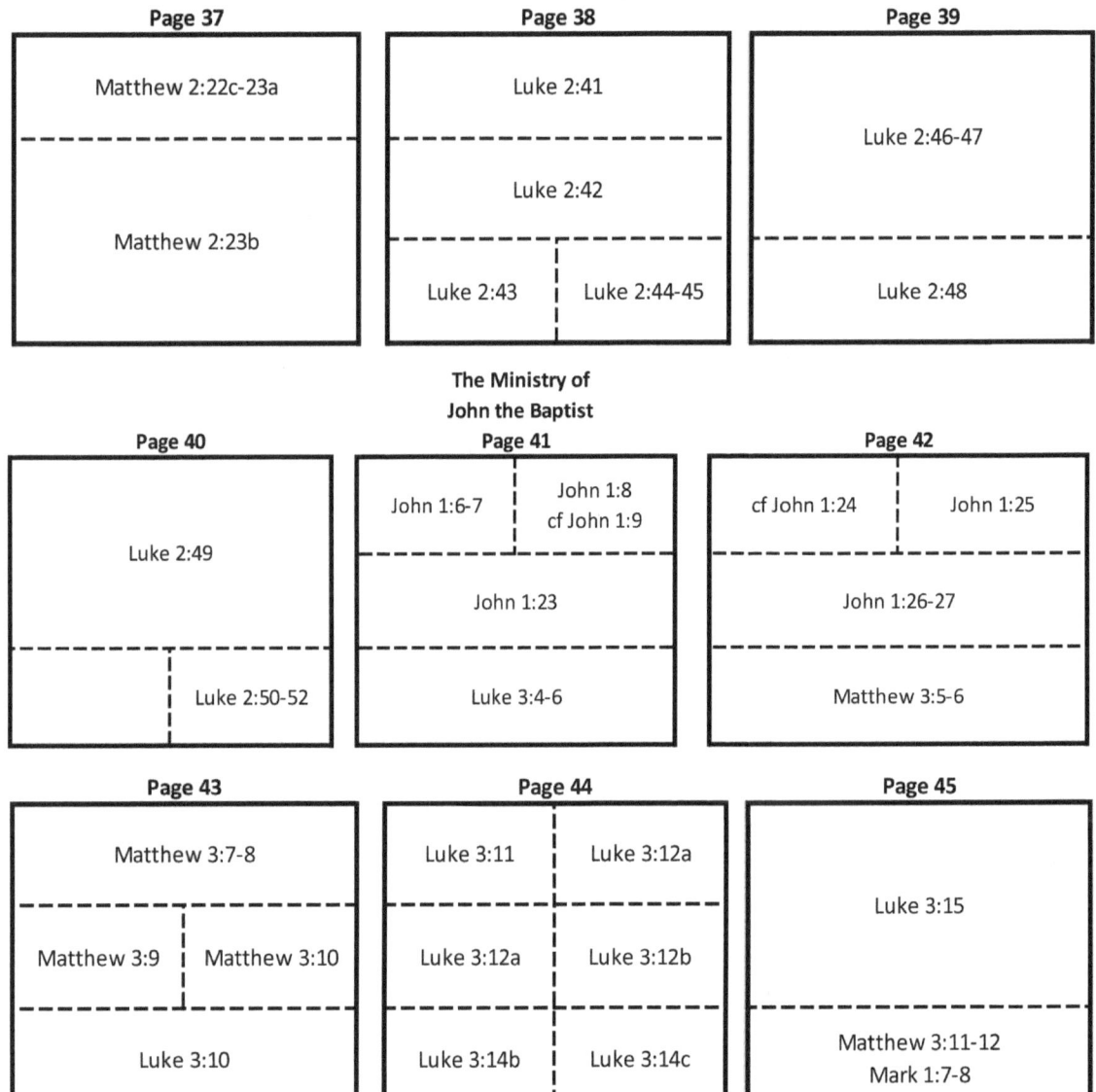

Appendix

The Joyful Gospel of Christ

When it is written that there is a particular author named to a Gospel that is not to say that person wrote the Gospel in question. In fact we do not know who first put pen to parchment.

Each of the Four Gospels comes from a different community with different needs. The prophet that God sent to each of the communities (Markan Community, Lucan Community, etc.) was asked about this Jesus person. The Evangelist told the people about Jesus, as the mouthpiece of God, and it was written down. Alternatively, just like the Apostle Paul, people may have written him with a problem of a lack of understanding. The Evangelist then wrote down "his" account of the Life of Jesus in a letter and it was sent to the community.

Luke for example, claims to be writing this of his own accord. We do not know why he was told to write in this way, but it has been theorized that it was him dictating to a scribe and the text begins in this way to reflect this. Furthermore, Luke as a physician would have been one to try and study the evidence, but came to faith in his analysis. Another possibility is that a scribe asked Luke about Jesus and wrote down everything that he said exactly how he said it. This would also explain the asides in some of the Gospels that explain the finer details to the audience.

Each one has a "style" that is indicative of the audience that was reached. Some communities knew about Judaic practices and others did not. These specifications were included so that the disciples could reach as many people as possible.

Each of the four Evangelists showed a different aspect of Christ. John focused on Christ's Divinity and puts more emphasis on the Godhead aspect of Jesus. Luke focused on the nature of Jesus as a servant and emphasizes Jesus serving others and how we are to imitate Him. Matthew writes about the humanity of Jesus and how Jesus was fully God, but put his focus on how Jesus was fully man. Mark wrote about Jesus as a king and speaks of the Davidic line.

This work combines all four Gospels into a single account. Each one focuses on different details for a different audience.

Sects in Judaism

The Pharisees, Sadducees, Essenes, and Zealots were the denominations of their day. Each one held to beliefs and traditions, but all of them worshipped The One True God. The Pharisees and the Sadducees were always at odds. They hated each other and could never agree. However, they both hated Jesus more.

The Pharisees were the common everyday people who did not have much money. They focused more on oral traditions of their own creation. They believed that ritual purity brought them closer to God and were more focused on the letter of the Law than the spirit of the Law.

Sadducees were made up of the wealthy and the Temple leaders that did not believe in The Resurrection. Jesus rarely interacted with these people.

The Essenes were a hermit-like sect that lived out in the wilderness that took ritual baths for the cleansing of sins. They are credited with writing the Dead Sea Scrolls and John the Baptist may have been a member.

The Zealots believed that the Romans should be outed by force. Simon the Zealot/Canaanite, a Disciple, is the only one that The Bible names.

Chapters
The Coming of John the Baptist

Theophilus is Greek for "Lover of God" or "One who loves God". Thus, Luke is writing this Gospel to the people of today as well.

A lot (lottery) is essentially putting all of the names of the people onto slips of paper and then drawing one out.

Appendix

This is where we first meet the messenger Angel Gabriel. There have been a lot of depictions of angels over the years. Most depictions of angels are not scripturally accurate and are based on Renaissance painters. However, no one knows what angels truly look like.

Prophetic books describe angels as having four heads or having a face of lightning. However, aside from these, there are few descriptions of angels.

In the New Testament, they are described as men in white garments. Thus angels are depicted here as ordinary men, but they glow and shine like the face of Moses. Their clothing is of whatever time and place they are in, but only of the purest white. The angels have greater radiance when speaking prophetically.

Zacharias doubted the angel, however the main problem with what he said was tone. The written word has neither tone nor inflection, save for punctuation. As such, the priest was sarcastic, crude, and insensitive and that is why God gave Gabriel the authority to silence him.

The Annunciation of Christ

Girls were often married as soon as they were able to bear children (12-14) and boys at about the same age. Many depictions put Mary and Joseph as much older than they should be.

The really big difference between Zacharias and Mary is her tone. Gabriel does not have nearly as much of a heavenly glow (save when prophesying) because Mary accepts his testimony. Mary is also confused by this Message. She does however accept what the angel tells her and so the difference was in tone and lacked sarcasm.

Cinematic depictions often depict Mary as middle-aged, but historically she would have been a young woman. People were married at a very young age in this era. Shorter lifespans affected the age of marriage.

The Visitation of Mary

Although many depictions show Mary as travelling by caravan, others have her travel with a small party.

There is an excellent example of culture in this section. If you look very closely at Elisabeth as she greets Mary, the table is very low to the ground. This is because people here actually sat on the floor around the table.

This section includes the Magnificat, the prayer that Mary speaks when Elizabeth comments on Mary coming to her as the mother of her Savior. Every step has been taken to ensure that it is as scripturally accurate as possible to ensure the reverence of Mary and the magnificence of the prayer.

The Birth of John the Baptist

It was traditional to name the first son after the father and the second son after the father's father. This is another reason that calling the child John was so controversial.

Zacharias would most likely have been using a reusable writing tablet. It is based on wet clay that would not be allowed to dry. When the book was closed, it would clear the writing surface to wipe the slate clean.

Zacharias has not said anything for nine months and when he is finally able to speak, he gives a wonderful sermon on The Love of God.

Zacharias mentions a "Horn of Salvation". In addition to sounding the alarm, horns were also used for anointing Kings. Samuel anointed David with a ram's horn.

Mary Returns to Nazareth

Because Joseph is quite young at this point, he was not given a full beard as he is often depicted with in order to keep with the historical context. There is however, some debate as to the age of Joseph. Some theologians have depicted him as an old widower that God chose specifically to help Mary.

In those days, if a woman was found to be pregnant outside of wedlock, she would have been ostracized from the community. If it had not been for the angelic intervention through Joseph, Mary would have been stoned according to Jewish Law.

Appendix

Although the description of people seeing Mary and Joseph going to the priest is not found in the original text, it was included for context. It also explains a little bit more for those who are not as familiar with the story and the time period that it takes place in.

The Nativity of Our Lord

Jesus was not born in a manger because there was no room in the inn. Jesus was born in a manger because there was no room in the house. Inns did not exist in towns like this in the first century. There might have been inns along the main roads, but not in the towns. The young couple would have stayed with Joseph's relatives.

It was very common to bring animals in at night to protect them from both the elements and from thieves. Thus the young couple would have stayed in the first century equivalent of a garage.

The Presentation of Christ in The Temple

Mary and Joseph brought their sacrificial birds because they were very poor. God wrote His Law in such a way that even the poor could just go out and capture a bird to sacrifice without having to purchase a larger animal.

Simeon and Anna must have seen countless children every day, but The Holy Spirit told them in an instant that This Child was The One. Simeon prophesizes that a sword will pierce Mary's heart, this would happen at the Crucifixion.

The Magi Adore Christ

There is no scriptural indication that the Magi were kings, they were merely wise men.

The devil has been depicted in many ways over the millennia. Also as a stylistic note, his name will not be captialized To be the most true to Scripture, satan is a fallen angel and would share traits in common with heavenly angels.

For this reason, the individual at Herod's side is a pale, sickly, and transparent figure. Gabriel and the rest of the Heavenly Court are strong and powerful, but satan has spent so much time away from God that he does not have as much strength. Furthermore, he also does not have the heavenly glow.

The Flight to Egypt

The Holy Family had to leave Bethlehem very quickly because the armies of Herod were getting ready. It is likely that Joseph was warned right after the Magi left to return to their own country.

This event is often called the Slaying of the Innocents.

Going all the way to Egypt was no easy feat. While Bethlehem and Jerusalem are right next door, Egypt was much further away.

Gold, frankincense, and myrrh were very expensive gifts. Since Joseph and his family had to pack light, these might have been their sole source of income during their journey and when they arrived in Egypt.

The Finding of Jesus in The Temple

While it might be typical to look down on Mary and Joseph for leaving their son in Jerusalem, this is not a fair complaint. Twelve years old was the age when boys started to become men. Since men and women traveled separately in caravans, Jesus could have been traveling with his mother or his father. Thus Mary and Joseph both thought that Jesus was with the other.

After the two find Jesus, and He declares being about His Father's Business and the priests are noticeably shocked. In saying this, Jesus is not only rejecting Joseph as His father, but is also claiming divinity. Perhaps since He was considered not quite an adult, the religious leaders just chose to ignore this.

The Ministry of John the Baptist

This is the first big parallel passage. This means that the same event is recorded amongst more than one Gospel, each with varying levels of detail. The reason that these events are so controversial is that they each appear to give details that the others leave out. Some

Appendix

biblical scholars have even proposed that the events are not how they occurred, but mostly recreated at the whim of the evangelist.

This is not an event that takes place over the course of one day, but over several days. The Four Evangelists tell of the events, but the exact timing was irrelevant to The Almighty's plan for our Salvation. Recall that each of the Evangelists was writing to a particular audience and the sermon was different for every audience.

Day I
1. Introduction to John the Baptist -John 1:6-9
2. The disciples of the Pharisees are sent to ask John questions. -John 1:24-27
3. The questions are answered over the next few verses and this culminates with John quoting Isaiah. –Luke 3:4-6

Day II
1. John calls the Pharisees, who now choose to confront him personally, to a "Generation of Vipers" -Luke 3:7-9, Matthew 3:7-10
2. Tax collectors and soldiers are told how to obtain salvation. –Luke 3:10-14
3. The people wonder whether John is The Christ -Luke 3:15
4. John gives the first of two speeches that are recorded in the narrative. –Matthew 3:11-12

Day III (These events take place in the second volume, The Luminous Gospel of Christ)
1. John gives another speech. –Mark 1:7-8
2. Jesus approaches, possibly at the end of the line. –Matthew 3:13, Mark 1:11
3. John announces Jesus. –John 1:28-31
4. John tries to say that Jesus should baptize him. –Matthew 3:14,
5. Jesus prayerfully enters the waters.
6. The heavens open up. –Matthew 3:16-17, Mark 1:10-11, Luke 3:21-22
7. John relates the event to his disciples, because John knows that he will be arrested soon and he wants them to not fall away. –John 1:32-34

Day IV (These events take place in the second volume, The Luminous Gospel of Christ)
1. John tells of Jesus to his disciples. –John 1:35-37

Day V (These events take place in the second volume, The Luminous Gospel of Christ)
1. John is arrested. –Luke 3:19

Thus, there is no contradiction in any passage found in Scripture.

Index

Aaron 1

Abraham 14

Angel 3, 4, 7, 8, 9, 10, 20, 21, 23, 24, 34, 35,

Anna 29

Baptism 41, 42, 44, 45

Bethlehem 22, 32, 34, 35

Betrothal (see marriage) 6

Caesar 22

Circumcise 15

David 20

Doctors 31, 32, 39, 40

Egypt 34, 35

Elders (see doctors)

Elisabeth 1, 2, 6, 11, 12, 15, 18

Gabriel 3, 4, 7, 8, 9

Galilee 30, 31

Herod, King 30, 31, 32, 33, 34, 35, 36

Holy Spirit/Holy Ghost 9

Isaiah 41

Israel 36

Jerusalem 30, 31, 38, 39, 42

John the Baptist 12, 15, 16, 18, 19, 41, 42, 43

Jordan 42

Joseph 6, 20, 21, 22, 23, 26, 34, 35, 36, 38, 39

Juda/Judea 11, 19, 42

King 9, 22, 30,

Marriage 6, 20, 21

Mary, Virgin 6, 7, 8, 9, 10, 11, 12, 13, 20, 21, 22, 25, 26, 27, 29, 33, 34, 35, 36, 38, 39,

Nazareth 6, 20, 37

Pharisees 42, 43

Priest 2, 31, 32

Rome/Romans 35, 45

Scribes (see elders)

Shepherd 23, 24, 25

Simeon 26, 27, 28

Soldier 45

Tax Collector 44,

The Temple 2, 3, 4, 5, 26, 27, 28, 29, 39

Theophilus 1

Wise Men 30, 31, 32, 33

Zacharias 1, 2, 3, 4, 15, 16, 17, 18

www.ingramcontent.com/pod-product-compliance
Lightning Source LLC
Chambersburg PA
CBHW042247100526

44587CB00002B/55